Putting the Sun to Work

All the energy on earth begins with the sun. The sun gives us heat and light, wind and weather, fresh water, growing plants. It makes life possible. Energy from the sun does the big work, all over earth. Now we are learning to harness that vast energy to do people's work—to supplement other energy resources that are being used up.

This clear, delightfully illustrated book shows where the sun's energy comes from, how we are learning to harness that energy, and for what. Easy investigations demonstrate the principles of solar energy, how those principles are put to work, and their possibilities for future use.

PUTTING THE SUN TO WORK

By Jeanne Bendick

GARRARD PUBLISHING COMPANY
CHAMPAIGN, ILLINOIS

Library of Congress Cataloging in Publication Data

Bendick, Jeanne.
    Putting the sun to work.

    Includes index.
    SUMMARY: Discusses the principles, practicality, and
possibilities of using solar energy to do some of our
everyday work.
    1. Solar energy—Juvenile literature. [1. Solar
energy] I. Title.
TJ810.B45   333.7   78-6178
ISBN 0-8116-6111-3

Contents

1. What the Sun Can Do

It's a hot summer day, and you, your family, and friends decide to drive to the beach for a cookout.

When you get to the beach, the sand and the rocks are so hot that they hurt your bare feet. You put on sneakers in a hurry. The water is so bright and shining in the sun that you can hardly look at it.

While the charcoal fire is starting to burn in the cookout stove, everyone goes for a swim. The water feels good—warm at the top, but cooler down around your toes.

A little wind is blowing when you come out. The fire isn't quite ready for cooking yet, so you play tag or read.

For lunch there are hot dogs, corn, salad and rolls, sodas, fruit, and coffee for the adults. By the time the coffee water boils and the corn and hot dogs are cooked, all the bathing suits are dry. So are the towels spread out on the rocks, in the sun.

Lunch is good. Just as you are finishing, it starts to rain, so you pack up and run. But nobody minds the rain. It will cool things off.

At the same time you were having fun at the beach, work was being done. Energy from the sun was doing the work. Energy, in one form or another, does all the work in the world.

Heat energy from the sun dried the towels. It heated the sand and the rocks, the water and the air. It even made the rain and the wind. Heat from the sun does small work and big work, all over earth.

HOW THE SUN MAKES RAIN

1. The sun shines on earth, on land and water.
2. Heat from the sun *evaporates* water from all over earth. It pulls water vapor into the air.
3. Water vapor condenses into water drops to form clouds.
4. Water from clouds rains on earth.

HOW THE SUN MADE THE WIND AT THE BEACH

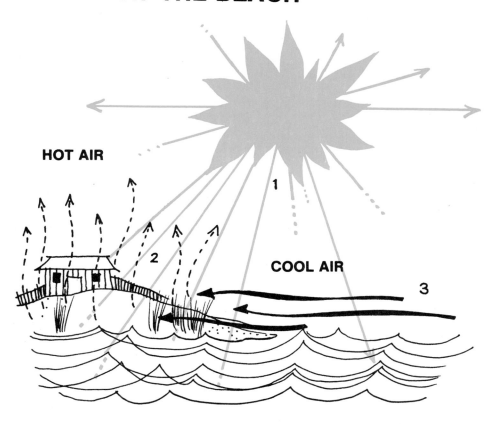

1. The sun shines on the land and the water, but the land heats up faster.
2. Hot air rises away from the land.
3. Cool air from over the water moves in to take its place. Moving air is wind.

YOU CAN USE THE SUN'S HEAT TO MAKE FRESH WATER OUT OF SALT WATER.

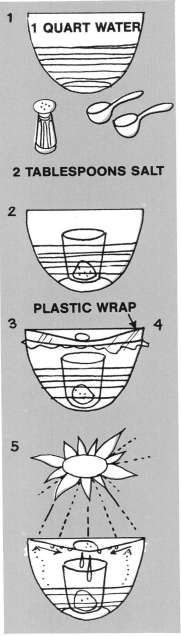

1 QUART WATER

2 TABLESPOONS SALT

PLASTIC WRAP

1. Put a quart of sea water in a bowl. If you have no sea water, make some by adding two tablespoons of salt to one quart of fresh water. (That is the average saltiness of sea water.)

2. Stand an empty glass in the middle of the bowl. (If the glass seems tippy, put a stone in it.)

3. Cover the bowl, but not too tightly, with a piece of plastic wrap. Fasten it around the bowl with a big rubber band.

4. Put a small stone or some other small, heavy object on the wrap, over the jar, like this, so that the wrap sags right over the glass.

5. On a hot, sunny day, put the bowl in the sun. After a while, drops of water will collect under the plastic wrap and roll down, inside, until they drip into the glass.

6. When enough has collected, taste the water in the glass. It may taste *brackish* (slightly salty), but it is all right to drink. Now taste the water in the bowl and compare the two. Is the water in the bowl saltier?

Light energy from the sun was working on the beach too. It supplied the daylight. It lit the earth and made the sand bright and the water sparkling.

The sun also supplied the energy that grew the food you ate.

Plants use light energy from the sun to make food for themselves. The food is a kind of sugar. It is also a kind of energy called chemical energy. Green plants change light energy from the sun into chemical energy.

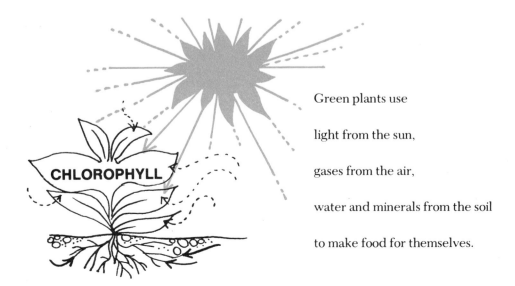

Green plants use

light from the sun,

gases from the air,

water and minerals from the soil

to make food for themselves.

Plants use some of that energy for everyday living and growing. They store the rest in their leaves and seeds, in fruit, roots, stems, and berries.

The salad and the corn, the rolls, fruit, and coffee all came from plants. You—and all animals—depend on plants for food.

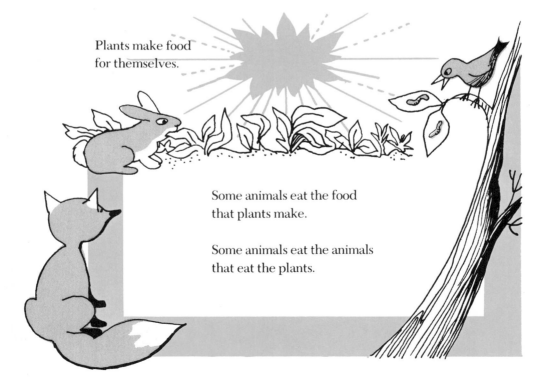

Plants make food for themselves.

Some animals eat the food that plants make.

Some animals eat the animals that eat the plants.

The charcoal you used for cooking began as a plant too. Once, that charcoal was a living tree that used sunlight to make food and then stored part of the food it made. The energy in this stored food remained, even after the tree died. You used that energy when you burned the charcoal.

A living tree has energy.

When the tree dies, that energy is still in the tree.

The gasoline you used for driving to the beach began with energy from the sun, too. It was made from oil.

Oil was formed from the remains of plants and animals that lived on earth millions of years ago. The remains of ancient living things are called fossils.

HOW FOSSIL FUELS ARE FORMED

1. Ancient plants and animals died

2. and were buried in the swamps, where
3. they decayed and sank deeper and deeper, under layers of later plants and animals, sometimes under new seas, sometimes under new rock.
4. Gradually they changed into pockets of coal, gas, and oil.

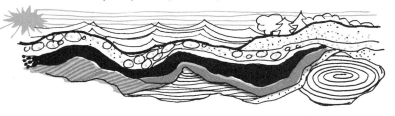

This is why oil is called a fossil fuel. Coal and natural gas are fossil fuels too.

Oil, coal, and natural gas all hold the chemical energy that was stored in those ancient plants, and in the animals that ate the plants. When you drive in a car, it is that stored energy that makes the car go.

Fossil fuels are easy to use. They are easy to store. They are easy to change into other forms of energy— heat, light, motion, electricity. They are so handy that people in many places around the earth use fossil fuels to supply almost all the energy they need.

Now fossil fuels are beginning to be used up. That's why people worry about running out of energy.

But as long as the sun shines, the earth will not run out of energy. The sun pours more energy on earth than we can ever use. Most of that energy comes to us as heat and light. Energy from the sun is called solar energy.

Anything to do with the sun is called "solar." The word began with the Roman word for the sun and their god of the sun, who was called Sol.

Solar energy is a safe kind of energy. It doesn't make pollution or have dangerous leftovers. That is why

scientists and inventors are experimenting with ways of harnessing the sun to
do some of the jobs fossil fuels have
been doing.

But to make the sun do work like
that, they have to solve some prob-
lems.

They have to collect the sun's
energy. Collecting sunshine isn't easy,
unless you are a plant.

Sunshine isn't easy to store, either.
You can't fill a tank with it or put it
in the woodbox. You can't move it
through a pipe or a wire. You can't
just turn it on.

Still, people have been using solar
energy to help do their work for a
long time. There are old ways and
new ways of catching sunshine and
putting it to work.

2. Catching Sunshine

Suppose you were living in a cold place and going to spend the winter in a cave. Would you choose a cave that faced the winter sun or a cave that faced away from it?

You might make the same choice if you were building a house in a cold place. You would probably build the house so the winter sun would pour in the windows to warm it. People have been building houses that way for a long time.

Is it possible to catch still more of the sun's heat in a house? Yes. Some houses also collect heat on the roof, move it indoors, store some, use some to make hot water and the rest for heating. A house like that is called a solar house.

Since prehistoric times the Indians of the Southwest have built their pueblos to catch the winter sun.

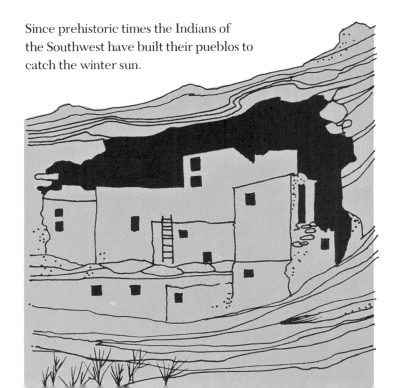

People who build solar houses have learned how to do those things by observing how the earth itself uses solar energy.

Remember the beach?

Remember the hot sand and the hot rocks?

Some materials take in heat energy from the sun and hold it. They absorb the heat. Sand and rocks do this. So do some other solid materials, such as metals. Water absorbs the sun's heat too.

Color can also be important. Dark, dull colors absorb heat. Light-colored, shiny surfaces reflect heat. They bounce it back. That's why dark clothes are warmer in the winter and light-colored clothes are cooler in the summer.

Water absorbs heat.

Dark colors absorb heat.   Light colors reflect heat.

The longer it takes something to heat up, the longer that thing holds the heat. Materials that heat up fast cool off fast.

If you go back to the beach in the evening after sunset, the sand and the rocks, which heated up fast, will be cool. But the water, which heated up slowly, will still be warm.

All through the summer, water absorbs the sun's heat slowly. Heat from the warmer air moves into the cooler water.

It takes a long time for the sun to heat the water in a big lake or the ocean. But by the end of summer, a large body of water will have caught and stored enough heat from the sun to last for a good part of the winter. Water stores heat very well.

That's why land near a large body of water never gets quite as cold in

In the winter, water gives back its
stored heat to the cooler air around it.

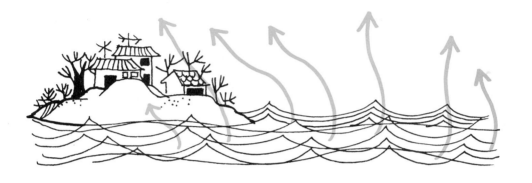

the winter as land far away from the
water. The stored heat in the water
keeps the land around it warm.

Slowly, all winter long, heat from
the water moves out into the cold air.
Heat always moves that way—from a
warmer place or thing to a cooler
one. Once you know which way heat
moves, you understand how things get
hot and how they lose heat.

Remember when the hot sand on the beach burned your feet? Heat from the sand was moving into your cooler feet!

Remember when you put the pot of water on the hot cookout stove? Heat moved from the stove into the pot and heated the pot. Then heat from the pot moved into the cool water and heated the water. Heat moved out of the water in the pot to heat the air. If you stop adding heat to the water in the pot, the water will go on giving off its heat until that water is the same temperature as the air around it.

Once you understand how heat moves into things, through things, and out of things, it is easy to see how a solar house works.

HOW A SOLAR HOUSE WORKS

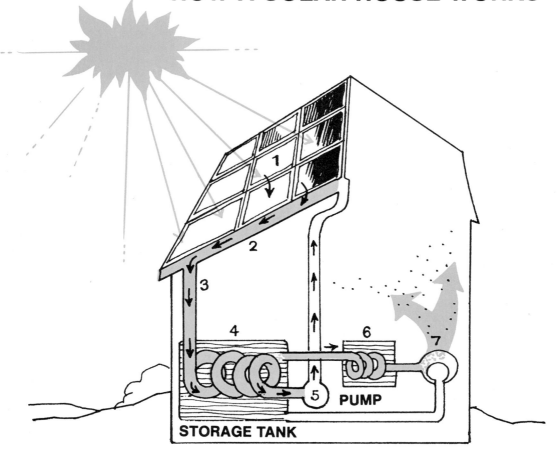

1. Sunshine is absorbed by flat pieces of black metal on the roof of the house. The metal on the roof gets hot.
2. The sun's heat moves from the roof into a liquid in pipes just under the metal. The liquid gets hot.
3. The hot liquid flows into a big pipe, into the house.
4. The pipe passes through a tank that stores water. The liquid stays in the pipe, but its heat moves through the pipe into the water in the tank. The water absorbs the heat and holds it.
5. When the liquid in the pipe has lost its heat, it is pumped back to the roof to be reheated by the sun.
6. Some of the heated water is used as hot water for the house.
7. Some of the water's heat warms the air in the house.

Some solar houses have tons of pebbles or crushed rock around the water storage tank to help hold the heat. Rocks hold heat better than air. Now scientists are experimenting with a special kind of rock salt that seems to hold the heat best of all.

In warm places around the earth, where there is a lot of sunshine, a solar house can supply all the heat and hot water most families need. But a solar house in a cold climate usually has some kind of backup heater to use if the weather is very cold or if the sun does not shine for some days.

Once the house is warm, what keeps the heat from moving out of the warm house into the cool outside air?

Remember the sneakers you put on when the hot sand was burning your feet? They kept the heat from moving from the sand into your feet. The sneakers were insulation. Insulation is any material that keeps heat (or other

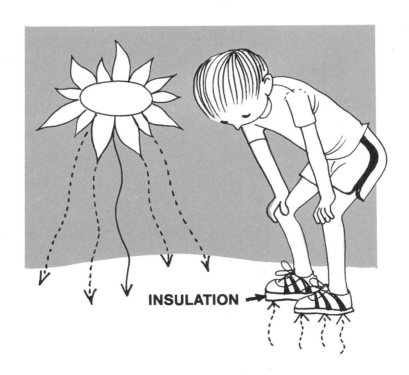

INSULATION →

kinds of energy) from moving from place to place.

Insulation in a house keeps heat from moving out of the house in the winter and into the house in the summer.

It does not take a great deal of heat to make a house comfortable. Solar energy can do that job in many places. But what about work that takes more heat, such as cooking dinner? Or still more, such as melting steel?

Can the sun do work like that?

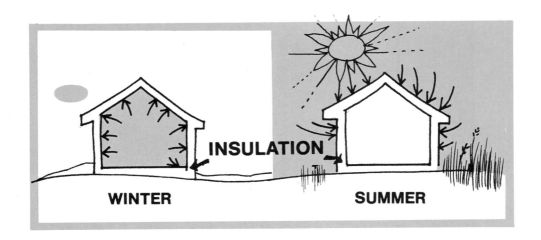

INSULATION

WINTER   SUMMER

3. Pulling Sunshine Together

If you have some burning sticks scattered around in a campfire, they won't give much heat. But if you gather those sticks together in one heap—if you *concentrate* them—they will give enough heat to keep you warm and cook your supper.

In a way, sunshine is like those scattered sticks. A huge amount of sunshine falls on earth, but it's spread out. Not much falls on one spot.

When sunshine is spread out, its heat is spread out too. No one spot gets much heat. But if the spread-out sunshine can be concentrated onto one spot, that spot will get hotter and also brighter.

All sunshine has light energy and heat energy. You can't really separate them. When you concentrate one, you concentrate the other.

Maybe it is only a story, but there is an old report that in 212 B.C. the great Greek scientist, Archimedes, used a bank of mirrors to concentrate the sun's light and heat on the sails of some Roman ships that were attacking his city.

The story says that the concentrated light and heat set fire to the sails and saved the city. According to the

legend, Archimedes caught the sun's
rays in his mirrors and then aimed
them at the Roman ships. He could
do that because all shiny surfaces
reflect light. If the light is sunlight,
they also reflect the heat that is part
of sunlight.

Long before there were telegraphs or telephones, people sent messages by bouncing sunlight off a shiny surface. The reflected light could be aimed in different directions and seen over long distances.

YOU CAN USE SUNLIGHT TO SIGNAL.

You can exchange signals with a friend who is out of sight by reflecting and aiming sunlight, like this.

The only equipment you need is a small mirror for each of you. By turning the mirror you can aim the sunlight in different directions.

(*Never* look directly at the sun.)

YOU CAN USE SUNLIGHT TO MAKE HEAT.

(You might need a friend to help you with this one. It's a little hard to do without three hands.)

1. Take two mirrors. See if you can catch the sunlight in both of them.
2. Aim the reflected light of both mirrors at a piece of black paper, on a table or on the ground.
3. Adjust the mirrors so that the reflected bright spots from both mirrors are one over the other.
4. Feel the bright spot on the paper in five minutes or so. How does it feel? Even on a cold winter day, the spot will be hot.
5. Try reflecting sunlight onto a white paper, too. Where is the heat this time? Is it above the paper?

Concentrating and aiming the sun's light and heat with shiny surfaces shows you how solar cookers work. There are many kinds of solar cookers.

One kind of solar cooker is made with flat, shiny reflectors, which aim the sunshine they catch onto the top of a black-painted metal box.

The reflectors concentrate the sunshine on the top of the box, which absorbs the heat. The food to be cooked is placed inside the box. Enough heat moves into the box to cook almost anything.

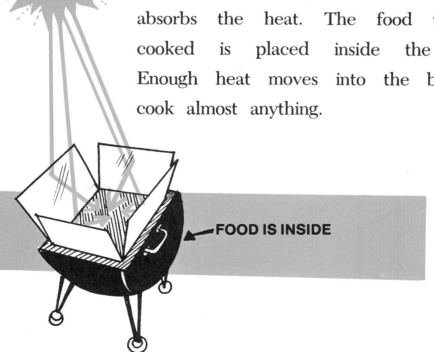

FOOD IS INSIDE

Shiny, flat surfaces gather and reflect sunshine, but a shiny curved surface does that even better.

A curved surface like the bowl of a spoon is called a parabola.

YOU CAN COLLECT A *LOT* OF SUNSHINE.

1. Take a big, shiny cooking spoon and hold it so the inside of the spoon reflects the sunlight.
2. Now hold a small piece of paper on a thin stick in front of the spoon.
3. You will see the curved surface of the spoon gather the sunlight and reflect it onto the paper in a small, bright spot. You have *focused* many beams of sunlight onto that spot. If you hold the spoon and paper long enough, the spot will get quite hot.

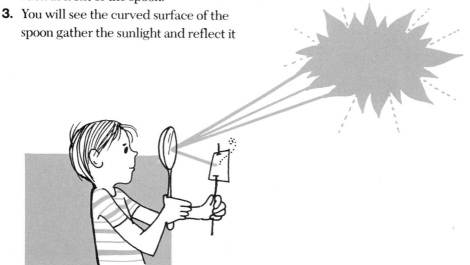

Most solar cookers are made with parabolas. You can make one too.

YOU CAN USE THE SUN FOR COOKING.

1. Start with a piece of cardboard you can bend.
2. Cover the cardboard with kitchen foil, shiny side out. Use rubber cement to hold the foil flat to the cardboard.
3. Bend the cardboard into a parabola, like this. Tie it into position with a thin piece of string.

SHINY SIDE OF FOIL

4. On a sunny day, break an egg into a tinfoil pieplate or small dish. Put it in the parabola, where the sunlight is focused on it. (You may have to use books under the plate to place it right.) Keep the sunlight focused on the egg. In the summer it will cook fast. Winter cooking will be slower.

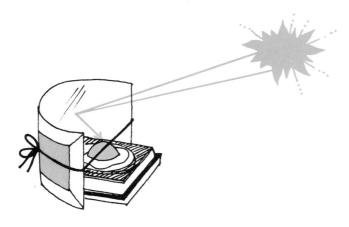

A solar cooker does not have to gather and focus a lot of heat to cook an egg or even a big piece of meat. But some work, like melting steel, requires an enormous amount of concentrated heat.

So does the testing of materials that have to stand extremely high temperatures. For example, the outside of a space capsule, coming back into earth's atmosphere, gets so hot that it glows. The safety of the astronauts

depends on how well the capsule stands that heat.

Big furnaces can do these big heat jobs. But most furnaces that can be heated to temperatures of thousands of degrees use huge amounts of fossil fuels.

There is another kind of furnace that can make heat like this without using fossil fuels. It uses energy from the sun and a giant parabola.

One solar furnace is in the mountains of France.

A solar furnace is much more powerful than your spoon parabola, but it works in just about the same way.

There are experimental solar furnaces in several places around the world. They collect and focus sunshine to do work where extreme heat is needed.

HOW A BIG SOLAR FURNACE WORKS

1. It has a reflector eight stories high, built of 9,500 tiny mirrors, arranged in a parabola.
2. Opposite the reflector, facing the sun, is a huge bank of large, flat mirrors, each about as tall as a person. These mirrors are controlled by a computer to follow the sun.
3. The sun shines onto the flat mirrors,
4. which reflect the sunshine onto the huge parabola.
5. The parabola gathers the sunshine and concentrates it into a single brilliant beam of enormous heat
6. and focuses the beam on a target. The beam is so powerful that it begins to melt steel in three seconds.

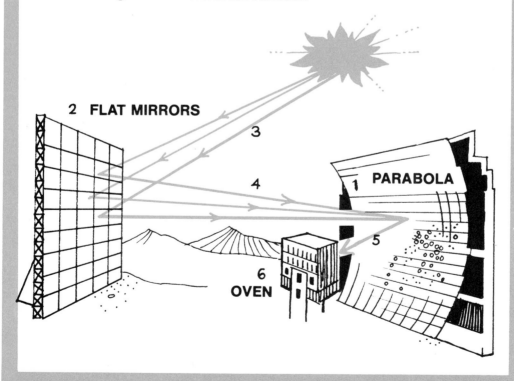

Smaller solar furnaces might be built in places where fuel—even wood—is scarce. Then the sun's heat could be used to do everyday work such as baking bricks and pottery. In other places small solar furnaces could do such hotter work as separating metal out of ore.

Solar furnaces could save a lot of fossil fuel. But nothing would save as much as being able to use solar energy to make electrical energy. Electricity is a very useful form of energy.

4. Changing Sunshine into Electricity

If you have ever been through a power blackout, you know how useful electricity is. It would be hard to do without electricity, in your house or in your town or city.

What makes electricity so useful? It can easily be changed into other forms of energy.

Electricity can be changed into heat, to cook a dinner or warm a house.

Electricity can be changed into

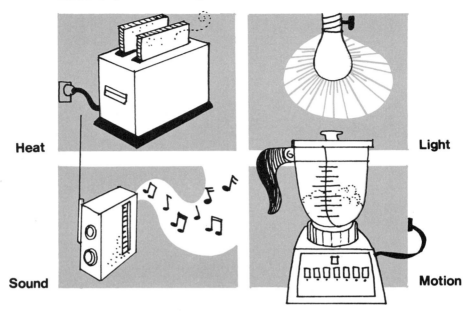

Heat

Light

Sound

Motion

Electricity can be changed into the energy of motion, to run a train, an elevator, or a blender.

Electricity can be changed into radio waves and sent through the air to your TV set where it is changed into sound and light.

All energy can be changed like that. One form can be changed into another to do a particular job.

Most power plants change the stored energy in fossil fuels into electricity by burning the fuel.

HOW FOSSIL FUEL MAKES ELECTRICITY

1. The burning fuel heats water in a boiler until it turns to steam.
2. The steam turns a turbine wheel.

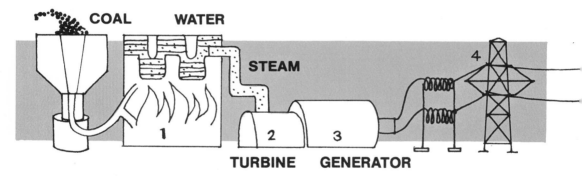

3. The wheel turns a coil inside a magnet in a generator.
4. Electricity comes out of the generator coil and flows through wires.

All over the world, people use electricity to do many kinds of work. It takes a lot of fossil fuel to make all that electricity.

HOW WATER POWER MAKES ELECTRICITY

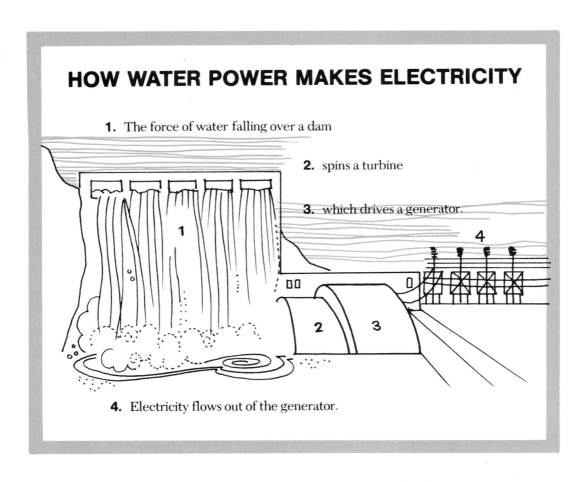

1. The force of water falling over a dam

2. spins a turbine

3. which drives a generator.

4. Electricity flows out of the generator.

There are other ways to make electricity.

Water power makes some.

But water power isn't everywhere.

Wind power makes some.

But the wind doesn't always blow.
Solar energy can make electricity too. And that's fine, because the sun never stops shining. You can't see it at night, or on a rainy day, but it is out there in space, shining.

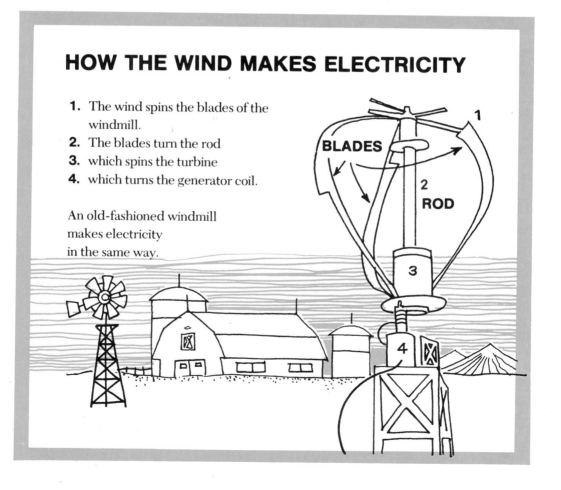

HOW THE WIND MAKES ELECTRICITY

1. The wind spins the blades of the windmill.
2. The blades turn the rod
3. which spins the turbine
4. which turns the generator coil.

An old-fashioned windmill makes electricity in the same way.

BLADES

1

2
ROD

3

4

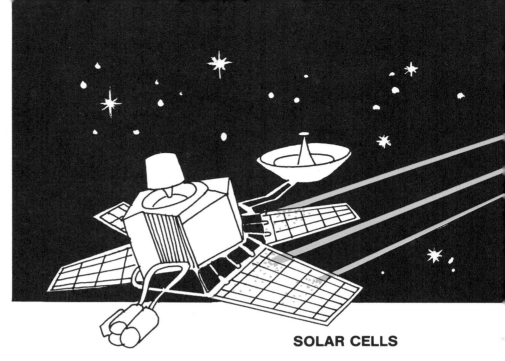

SOLAR CELLS

Space is always black because
there is no air to reflect sunlight.

Have you ever heard of solar cells?
Solar cells supply the electricity that
runs the instruments in space satellites.

Space satellites are out past the
earth's atmosphere. There are no
cloudy or rainy days because there is
no air and no water. And since the
turning earth makes day and night,
there is no night.

48

Solar cells generate electricity when sunlight shines on them. A solar cell doesn't need any fuel except sunlight. There is no big machinery and no pollution, heat, or noise. Solar cells are a fine way to make electricity. But the problem is that there is no easy way to make solar cells.

Solar cells are made from a mineral called silicon. Silicon is very common, but it is always found combined with other materials, and that's part of the problem. A solar cell must be made from *pure* silicon. Making pure silicon crystals, then cutting them into thin, thin chips takes a long time and is very expensive.

HOW A SOLAR CELL MAKES ELECTRICITY

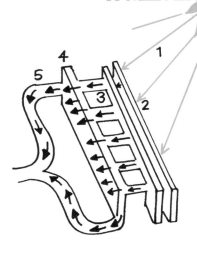

1. Energy from the sun
2. falls on a thin slice of silicon, heating it up.
3. This makes electrons in the silicon jump out of that slice into a connected slice of silicon. Electrons are electricity.
4. The second slice of silicon now has extra electrons, and they have to move on. Extra electrons, moving freely, become electric current when they move together.
5. The extra electrons flow out of the solar cell as electric current.

A solar cell is a sort of sandwich of two thin slices of silicon.

One solar cell makes only a tiny bit of electric current. But if enough solar cells are connected, they make enough to be really useful.

50

Scientists are trying to find easier, cheaper ways to make solar cells. Until they do, solar cells can be used only for special jobs.

They supply electricity to out-of-the-way, hard to reach places, usually where there are no power lines.

Solar cells are dependable. They work for months and years without needing to be repaired or replaced.

They operate the lights and the sound signals on the buoys that guide sailors at sea.

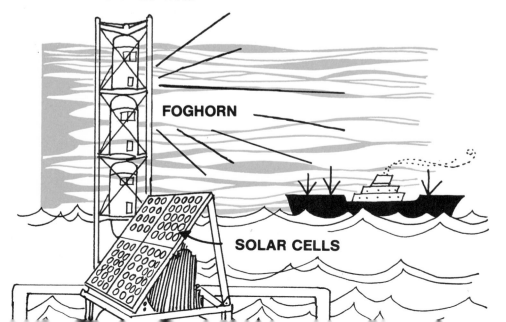

FOGHORN

SOLAR CELLS

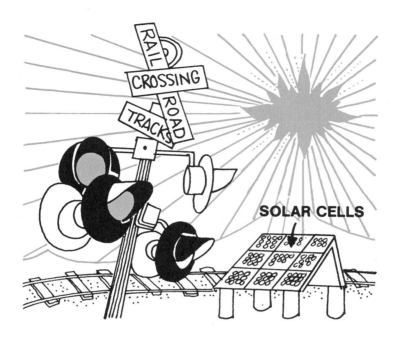

They run the instruments in weather stations and radio and television relay stations on the tops of high mountains or far out in the desert.

They operate railway signals and roadside call boxes.

They run the instruments in space satellites.

Far out in space, the sun is always shining. Scientists think that some day huge power stations might operate in space, more than 22,000 miles out from earth. Each one would have billions of solar cells changing sunlight into electricity.

HOW A SOLAR POWER STATION WOULD WORK

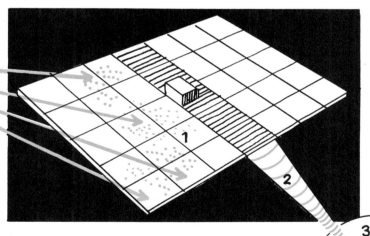

1. Miles of solar cells would change sunlight into electricity.
2. The electricity would be changed into radio waves and beamed to earth.
3. Giant receiver stations would change the radio waves back to electricity, which would flow out through wires.

The electricity would be changed into a kind of radio waves called microwaves, which would be beamed to huge receivers on earth. The receivers would change the microwaves back into electricity.

Scientists think that 120 satellites out in space could make all the electrical energy people would need, all over earth. But it will be a long, long time before that is possible.

Another way of changing solar energy into electricity uses concentrated sunshine, the way it is used in a solar furnace.

A solar energy "power tower" is located in the desert, where there is sunshine almost all day, every day.

HOW A POWER TOWER WOULD WORK

1. Thousands of curved mirrors are arranged around the tower.
2. Computers keep the mirrors moving so that they reflect the sun all day.
3. The beams from all the mirrors are concentrated on a boiler at the top of the tower. Their heat makes steam in the boiler.
4. The steam turns a turbine that turns the coil in a generator that makes electricity.
5. The electric current flows out of the generator through wires.

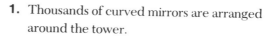

BOILER

3

STEAM

TURBINE

4

GENERATOR

4

5

5

2

2

1

2

Some people say that the sun can never supply more than 20% of the energy that people need.

Some people say that scientists and inventors will find ways of harnessing the sun to supply all the energy people can ever use to do their work.

Whoever is right, one thing is sure. We will be using more solar energy. But it doesn't matter how much we use, because it's one kind of energy we can never use up. The sun keeps making more.

Where does the sun get all that energy?

5. Inside the Sun

When you feel the sun's heat or use its light, you are feeling and using energy that has traveled 93 million miles through space.

This energy begins deep inside the sun, where the heat and pressure are greater than anything you can imagine.

The sun isn't solid, as the earth is. It is a huge, lumpy, flaming ball,

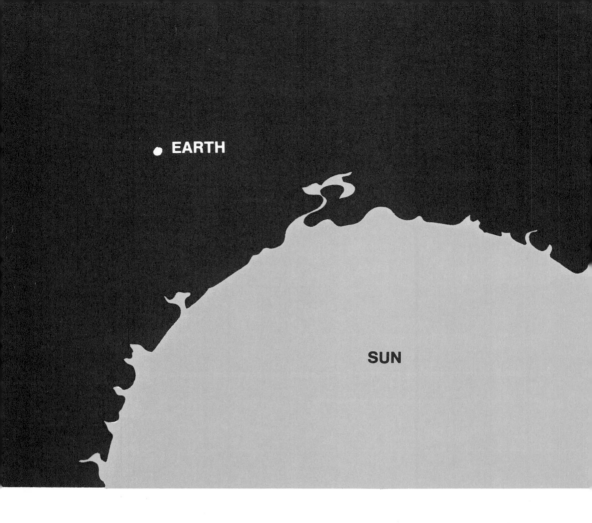

EARTH

SUN

made mostly of the gases hydrogen and helium. When the sun, which is a star, is compared to other stars, the sun is only medium-sized. Compared to earth, the sun is very big. More than a million earths could fit inside it.

Scientists aren't sure, but they think that deep inside the sun, hydrogen atoms by the millions and trillions are being smashed together and changed into helium atoms. When that happens, bits of atoms fly out as energy.

HYDROGEN ATOM

HELIUM ATOM

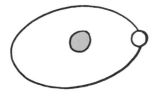
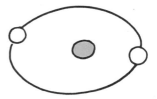

When two hydrogen atoms are smashed together, something is left over.

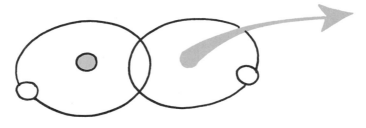

That left-over bit of atom flies out of the new atom as energy.

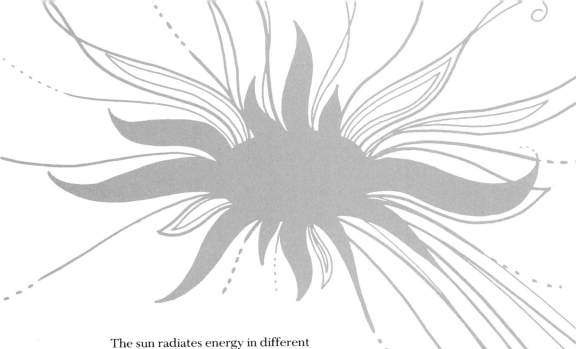

The sun radiates energy in different forms — light, heat, ultraviolet rays, radio waves, X-rays.

It takes thousands of years for the energy that is made deep inside the sun to reach the surface of the sun, where it flies out into space.

The sun gives off several kinds of energy, but the most important ones to us are heat and light.

Energy from the sun travels out into space in all directions. Heat radiates

away from the sun the way heat radiates away from a radiator. Light radiates away from the sun the way light
radiates away from a light bulb.

Only a small part of all the sun's
energy reaches earth.

Some energy is lost in the 93-
million-mile journey through space.

Some is lost passing through the
earth's atmosphere. Some is absorbed.
Some is reflected back into space by
air and water vapor in the air.

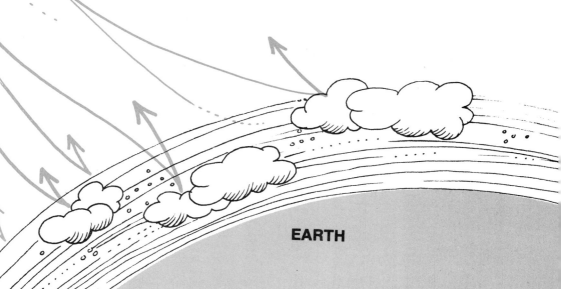

EARTH

Some of the sunshine that gets through the atmosphere is reflected away from earth by the shiny surfaces of water and of snowy, icy places on land.

Some of the sunshine that falls on earth is absorbed by oceans and lakes and by rocks and soil.

But even so, more energy falls on earth in a few minutes than people everywhere use in a year.

Energy from the sun will always do the big work on earth—heating it, moving the air and water, supplying energy to plants. What we need is to find better ways to make solar energy do the smaller work—people's work.

Index